I0012197

The Birth of Hybrid AI

Combining Machine and Human
Intelligence

Table of Contents

1. Introduction 1

2. The Dawn of a New Era: An Introduction to Hybrid AI 2

    2.1. The Emergence of Hybrid AI 2

    2.2. Hybrid AI: Bridging the Gap 3

    2.3. Hybrid AI and Human-Machine Synergy 3

    2.4. Limitations and Overcoming Challenges 3

    2.5. Beyond the Horizon: The Future of Hybrid AI 4

3. First Generation AI: Predecessors to Hybrid Systems 6

    3.1. The Roots of Intelligence: Turing and His Test 6

    3.2. Symbolic AI: Logic and Reasoning Systems 7

    3.3. Expert Systems: The Pioneers of Decision-making AI 7

    3.4. The Emergence of Machine Learning 8

    3.5. The Advent of Neural Networks 8

4. Birth of the Idea: Human-Machine Interworking 10

    4.1. The Conceptual Underpinnings 10

    4.2. Early Development and Progress 11

    4.3. Realizing the Full Potential 12

5. The Cogs and Gears: Understanding Technology Behind Hybrid
AI 14

    5.1. The Conceptual Framework 14

    5.2. Core Technologies Behind Hybrid AI 15

        5.2.1. Data Acquisition and Preprocessing 15

        5.2.2. Machine Learning Algorithms 15

        5.2.3. Deep Learning Architectures 16

        5.2.4. Natural Language Processing Techniques 16

        5.2.5. Human Involvement and Integrative Processing 16

    5.3. Tools and Technologies 16

6. Building Bridges: Harmonizing Machine Logic and Human

Reasoning 18
   6.1. The Theory of Cognition and Computation 18
   6.2. Decoding the Human Brain: Neuroscientific Insights into
   Cognition 19
   6.3. The Arithmetic of Reasoning: Transposing Cognition onto
   Computation 19
   6.4. Rationalizing the Machine: Imparting Human-Like
   Reasoning 20
   6.5. The Machine-Human Bridge: Hybrid AI 21
7. Diverse Facets: Applications of Hybrid AI in Modern World 22
   7.1. Commercial Applications of Hybrid AI 22
   7.2. Health and Medical Fields 23
   7.3. Education and Learning 23
   7.4. Defense and Cybersecurity 24
   7.5. Sustainability and Environmental Conservation 24
8. Case Studies: Successful Implementations of Hybrid AI 26
   8.1. Google's AlphaGo: A Revolution in Strategy Gaming . . . 26
   8.2. IBM's Watson: A Companion Physician 27
   8.3. Airbus's Skywise: Combining AI and Human Insights for
   Aviation Safety 27
   8.4. Automated Trading Systems: Financial Market Predictions . . 28
   8.5. Conclusion 28
9. Cyber Ethics: Contemplating the Moral Landscape of Hybrid AI . 30
   9.1. Exploring the Ethical Concerns 30
   9.2. Navigating in the Ocean of Data Privacy 31
   9.3. The Balance: Autonomy and Dependancy 31
   9.4. Inclusion and Accessibility 31
   9.5. The Ownership Dilemma 32
10. Future Potential: Exploring the Uncharted Terrains of Hybrid
AI 33

10.1. Evolution of AI: From Traditional to Hybrid 33

10.2. Machine Learning and Reasoning: The Dynamic Duo 34

10.3. Human-AI Collaboration: Co-Existence and Co-Evolution . . . 34

10.4. Multidimensional AI Scaling: Addressing the Complexity
of Reality 35

10.5. Imagining Scenario-Specific Explorations 35

    10.5.1. Healthcare: Crafting Healthier Tomorrows 35

    10.5.2. Education: Personalizing Wisdom 36

    10.5.3. Business: Reinventing Industries 36

10.6. Embracing Challenges: Understanding Limitations 36

11. Conclusion: The Journey Ahead in the Hybridized AI
Landscape 38

11.1. Synergizing Human and Machine Intelligence 38

11.2. Unleashing the Potential of Hybrid AI 39

11.3. Uncharted Horizons and Unforeseen Challenges 39

11.4. Embracing Hybrid AI as an Imperative for Future
Innovation 40

Chapter 1. Introduction

In the world of innovation, the marriage of two unlikely entities can often yield extraordinary outcomes. Such is the case with the birth of Hybrid Artificial Intelligence (AI), a fascinating convergence of machine intelligence and human intellect that is revolutionizing the way we interact with technology. Despite the technicality of the subject, our Special Report seeks to unfold this complex panorama in an approachable and relatable manner. The report offers a comprehensive understanding of Hybrid AI, illustrating its inception, development, applications, and potential future in plain and comprehensible terms. By delving into this report, you'll gain a refreshing perspective on AI that very well might change the way you perceive this breathtaking hybrid of human and machine intellect. The birth of Hybrid AI is more than a technological innovation- it is a passage into previously unventured realms of possibility, ready to be discovered by you.

Chapter 2. The Dawn of a New Era: An Introduction to Hybrid AI

The genesis of artificial intelligence (AI) emerges from the quest for achieving complex tasks with relative ease, catalyzing proficiency and productivity. With the entry of Hybrid AI, a miraculous blend of machine intelligence and human intellect, this quest is taking an entirely new form and direction.

Understanding Hybrid AI requires a historical reference point, a comprehension of traditional AI, and an acknowledgment of its limitations. Traditional AI systems were designed to mimic human intelligence, performing tasks such as understanding natural language, recognizing patterns, problem-solving, and learning. Yet, these machines were fundamentally limited by algorithmic rigidity. Despite their complex data processing abilities, understanding context, emotions and subtleties of human interaction remained beyond their grasp.

2.1. The Emergence of Hybrid AI

This persistent challenge prompted the inception of Hybrid AI, a new era in technological innovation. Hybrid AI is an amalgamation of machine intelligence and human intellect, producing smarter, contextual, empathetic, and intuitive AI systems. By synergizing the best of both worlds, Hybrid AI expands the spectrum of possibilities, making artificial intelligence more relatable and intuitive.

Unlike the traditional AI approach, which is entirely algorithm-driven, Hybrid AI involves incorporating cognitive architecture into the machine's systems. Cognitive architecture is a type of artificial intelligence that mimics human thought processes and behavior. It includes elements of human intellect like perception, attention, motor control, learning, and memory. By doing so, Hybrid AI achieves a level of sophistication and context-awareness unseen in previous AI models.

2.2. Hybrid AI: Bridging the Gap

The most striking attribute of Hybrid AI is the potent way it bridges the gap between human-like intelligence and artificial systems. The system is designed to learn and adapt to change dynamically, just like humans. It can interpret unstructured data, solve unforeseen problems, and even react to emotional cues, making human-machine interplay seamless and more engaging.

2.3. Hybrid AI and Human-Machine Synergy

A heartening aspect of Hybrid AI is its potential to foster increased cooperation between humans and technology. This is achieved through so-called augmented intelligence, where AI operates as a comrade rather than a commander. Hybrid AI doesn't just automate tasks but enhances human decision-making by providing data-driven insights, thus creating a synergy between human intuition and machine capabilities.

2.4. Limitations and Overcoming Challenges

Despite its impressive credentials, Hybrid AI is not without its limitations and obstacles. The complexity of human cognition, ethical considerations around AI, and resistance to change pose significant challenges. However, these are not insurmountable. By continuing to refine the algorithms, developing robust ethical guidelines, and educating the public and corporations about the benefits of Hybrid AI, these hurdles can be overcome, paving the way for a more interconnected and accessible technological world.

2.5. Beyond the Horizon: The Future of Hybrid AI

With the latest advancements, the future of Hybrid AI holds promises of more precise algorithms, nuanced machine behaviors, and enhanced compatibility with human users. It stands at the dawn of a new era, set to revolutionize various industries - from healthcare to education, commerce to politics. It is primed to not only redefine the way we interact with technology but also reimagine the way we perceive reality itself.

At the core of this transformation lies the belief that the integration of artificial and human intelligence can bring monumental prosperity, facilitating a cognitive revolution. The journey ahead is permeated with exceptional potential and unexplored opportunities.

In conclusion, Hybrid AI, the convergence of machine intelligence and human intellect, is the dawn of a promising new era. This groundbreaking technology presents a whole new realm of possibilities, marking a significant departure from traditional AI systems. Sure, challenges remain, but the potential rewards in terms of efficiency, productivity, and enhanced human-machine interaction significantly outweigh the hurdles. As we move towards an increasingly digital future, Hybrid AI promises to be the bedrock of our technological evolution.

Demystifying this new era of Hybrid AI, understanding its complexities and capabilities, and exploring its potential, impacts all of us. There is little doubt that this next generation of AI will shape and define our future, playing an integral role as we tread into uncharted territories of possibility. Thus, reaffirming the importance of exploring Hybrid AI - not merely as an academic or technological pursuit, but as a fascinating new lens for envisioning our digital future.

Chapter 3. First Generation AI: Predecessors to Hybrid Systems

The emergence and progression of artificial intelligence is a tale of technological evolution that saw the shift from rudimentary algorithms to the development of increasingly agile and autonomic forms of cognition. Indeed, the journey begins long before the conjuring of what we now know as Hybrid AI, with the development of its predecessors: First Generation AI systems.

In order to fully grasp the concept and potential of Hybrid AI, it's imperative that we delve into the origins of its predecessors, their capabilities, and the role they have played in shaping the multidimensional nature of modern AI technology.

3.1. The Roots of Intelligence: Turing and His Test

Alan Turing, a British mathematician, is well-respected within the community as the forefather of theoretical computer science and artificial intelligence. His work was instrumental in changing the course of World War II, as he played a pivotal role in cracking notoriously complex coded messages, thereby disrupting the strategies of the enemy forces.

His monumental contribution to the field of artificial intelligence came in the form of the Turing Test. Designed to assess a machine's ability to exhibit intelligent behavior equivalent to, or indistinguishable from, that of a human, the test was the first of its kind to propose a criterion for machine intelligence.

3.2. Symbolic AI: Logic and Reasoning Systems

Symbolic AI, also known as "Good Old-Fashioned AI" (GOFAI), marked the inception of first-generation AI. Symbolic systems focussed on implementing human intellect's problem-solving and decision-making capabilities into machines.

These systems employed a rule-based approach where every constituent of knowledge was broken down into symbols. Complex problems were structured as symbolic expressions, and these symbols manipulated to signify reasoning and infer logic akin to human cognition. From solving mathematical theorems to playing chess, these systems showcased the ability to accomplish tasks perceived to be distinctive characteristics of intelligent beings.

3.3. Expert Systems: The Pioneers of Decision-making AI

Encouraged by the success of symbolic AI, researchers pushed the boundaries even further, leading to the development of so-called "Expert Systems". These were AI programs designed to provide solutions to complex problems in particular areas of expertise, replicating decision-making abilities akin to human experts in those fields.

Expert systems consisted of a knowledge base, which held extensive data in a specific field, and an inference engine, which applied logical rules to this knowledge base to extract useful information or conclusions. The most renowned example was MYCIN, a medical diagnostic system that showed early promise in diagnosing bacterial infections and suggesting appropriate antibiotic treatments.

3.4. The Emergence of Machine Learning

Despite the somewhat successful imitations of human-like cognition in tasks like problem-solving and decision-making, first-generation AI systems lacked the ability to learn from new data and consequently adapt their responses or reflexes. This shortcoming became particularly apparent when complex, real-world applications were concerned, leading to the advent of Machine Learning (ML).

ML models were designed to automatically learn and improve their performance from experience, instead of being explicitly programmed for each specific task. This breakthrough allowed systems to predict outcomes and make decisions with minimum human intervention, thereby automating a plethora of tasks that were impractically time-consuming for humans.

3.5. The Advent of Neural Networks

Drawing inspiration from biological brains, researchers conceptualized Artificial Neural Networks (ANNs) as a way of mimicking the interconnected structure of neurons to process information. The nodes in these networks, just like neurons, work collectively to carry out a range of tasks, including pattern recognition, decision making, and learning from experience.

Through back-propagation and optimization algorithms, ANNs were trained to improve their predictions over time, thereby demonstrating a form of learning inspired by biological organisms. However, they were limited by their shallow architectures, which could only handle linearly separable patterns due to the single layer between the input and output nodes.

It's important to understand that this journey of first-generation AI, from symbolic systems to neural networks, laid the groundwork for the development of later AI generations. These rudimentary AI forms set the precedent for the fusion of machine intelligence and human intellect, birthing Hybrid AI. Each step in the evolution of these systems highlighted the potential that AI carried, while underlining the need for more human-like adaptability, learning capabilities, and nuanced reasoning. As we explore further into the complexities and capabilities of advancing AI systems, remember that each innovation didn't just spring forth in isolation but emerged from the lessons, limitations, and leaps of understanding embodied by its predecessors.

Chapter 4. Birth of the Idea: Human-Machine Interworking

The genesis of the idea of Hybrid AI, which combines the prowess of machine intelligence with the sophistication of human intellect, mimics the nature of its creation: a remarkable marriage of two unlikely entities. Initially considered separate domains, artificial intelligence and human thought have now become intertwined, generating an exquisite melange that, while still in its embryonic stage, promises to redefine the landscape of technology and human interaction.

The inception of Hybrid AI can be traced back to the dawn of Artificial General Intelligence (AGI). AGI depicts a future where artificial systems harbor the potential to execute any task a human being is capable of. However, these visionaries often neglect the fact that the human brain is not just a logical processor but also an emotional, creative, and experiential being. It is within this context that the idea of Hybrid AI came into existence.

4.1. The Conceptual Underpinnings

Hybrid AI converges two seemingly divergent streams of thought: humanity's revered ability to imagine, interpret, and experience, and the straightforward efficiency and precision of machine learning algorithms. It discounts the idea of machines rivaling humans, instead fostering an environment where both coexist, collaborate, and complement each other. In essence, it is a synergized intersection of biological and artificial intelligence.

Unpacking the conceptual foundation of Hybrid AI necessitates understanding the strengths and abilities of both human and machine intelligence. Human cognition has evolved over millennia, enabling us to engage with complex emotions, comprehend nuances, generate creative ideas, make judgments, and acquire wisdom through lived experiences. However, humans are not immune to errors, forgetfulness, or biases, limitations that machines tend to overcome.

Machine intelligence has made technology ubiquitous and vital for contemporary life. However, while powerful at number crunching, pattern identification, and carrying out tasks with incredible speed and scale, machines lack the capability to comprehend or replicate human emotional intelligence and our highly nuanced sense of the world. Hybrid AI seeks to marry these diverse capabilities, creating an entity mixed with the strengths of both.

4.2. Early Development and Progress

The development of Hybrid AI systems kicked off with the amalgamation of Expert Systems and Machine Learning. Expert Systems encapsulated a set of rules, provided by human experts, that machines could follow. However, these machines lacked learning abilities; they could not update or improve with additional knowledge or experience.

With the advent of Machine Learning, this scenario changed dramatically. Machines not only learned from data but also improved their performance with experience. But, there was a limitation – while machines were excellent at recognizing patterns from vast swathes of data, they lacked contextual understanding. Hence, they were regularly stumped by situations not covered in the learning data or that required a degree of intuition or empathy.

Hybrid AI systems, by incorporating fuzzy logic and human input into machine learning frameworks, began to tackle some of these limitations. As a paradigm, Hybrid AI has been envisaged as a system where humans can teach, direct, and communicate with machines just as if they were colleagues.

4.3. Realizing the Full Potential

Hybrid AI's full potential crystallizes on multiple fronts. Firstly, it offers a solution to the limitations inherent in both human decision-making and machine intelligence. It combines the empathetic, creative, and wise decision-making faculty of humans with the accuracy, speed, and memory of AI. In essence, Hybrid AI can provide superior intellectual partnership, where human and AI work together to arrive at better decisions, predictions, and judgments.

Secondly, Hybrid AI can elevate technology from being a facilitating tool to an intellectual partner, having the potential to revolutionize the way we live, work, and create. Say, for example, a designer working on a new product; the Hybrid AI could comprehend the brief, interact with the designer, provide feedback, suggest modifications, or even inspire new design ideas. It can assist doctors in diagnosing and treating illnesses, help scientists make breakthrough discoveries, among countless other possibilities.

Finally, by augmenting human intellect rather than replacing it, Hybrid AI offers a reassuring vision of the future, contrary to the dystopian narrative often portrayed. It eliminates the competitive element often associated with AI and instead fosters a cooperative future where human and machine intellects complement each other.

The idea of Hybrid AI, thus, does not merely signal another evolution in the field of AI. It promises a path into previously uncharted territories where human beings and AI can blend seamlessly, offering innumerable exciting possibilities to be discovered and harnessed. The subsequent chapters will delve into how Hybrid AI is being applied across various domains and the potential challenges that need to be addressed to realize its full potential. Meanwhile, the

History of AI can help illuminate why Hybrid AI is considered a significant evolution in this field and its place in the broader narrative of AI development.

Chapter 5. The Cogs and Gears: Understanding Technology Behind Hybrid AI

Stepping behind the veil of hybrid Artificial Intelligence, we find ourselves amidst an intricate dance of algorithms, data processors, and intuitive programs. This union of artificial intelligence with human intellect could be likened to the unity of two infinities, yielding unforeseen possibilities at their convergence. It's a fitting background to begin to understand the machinery that facilitates this unique synthesis.

5.1. The Conceptual Framework

A meeting ground of machines and minds, Hybrid AI rests on the broad pillars of Machine Learning (ML), Deep Learning (DL), and Natural Language Processing (NLP). However, to truly grasp the technological ethos of Hybrid AI, we must delve into the specifics of these notions.

ML, at its core, is a data analysis method that employs an iterative approach to learn from data, enabling decisions and predictions based on experience. This methodology emancipates systems from explicit programming, enabling them to learn and improve performance with experience.

DL, a subset of ML, imitates the workings of the human brain in processing data for pattern identification. It employs artificial neural networks with several hidden layers to carry out the process of machine learning, thereby leading to a hierarchical interpretation of complex data.

NLP, meanwhile, facilitates computers' understanding,

interpretation, manipulation, and generation of human language, allowing more sophisticated interaction between human users and AI systems.

5.2. Core Technologies Behind Hybrid AI

Understanding the building blocks of Hybrid AI means delving into the technological specifics. We will dissect each technological component, unraveling the cogs and gears behind this captivating marvel.

5.2.1. Data Acquisition and Preprocessing

In the realm of Hybrid AI, data is the drive. Data acquisition involves collecting raw data from various sources to be used in ML algorithms, with the aim to teach the system to identify patterns and make decisions. On acquiring data, the critical task of preprocessing initiates. Here, the data undergoes processing to eliminate redundancy, reduce complexity, and strengthen the ML model's predictability.

5.2.2. Machine Learning Algorithms

Once processed, the data is run through ML algorithms. These algorithms are classified into three categories: supervised learning, unsupervised learning, and reinforcement learning.

In supervised learning, the model makes predictions based on a set of labeled examples. On the other hand, unsupervised learning has no labeled examples to learn from, hence it finds hidden patterns or intrinsic structures from the input data. In reinforcement learning, an agent learns to behave in an environment by performing certain actions and observing the results thereof.

5.2.3. Deep Learning Architectures

DL architectures leverage artificial neural networks. Three main types of DL architectures are employed in Hybrid AI - Feedforward Neural Networks (FNN), Convolutional Neural Networks (CNN), and Recurrent Neural Networks (RNN). These stand as the backbone of advanced image recognition, speech recognition, and natural language generation respectively.

5.2.4. Natural Language Processing Techniques

NLP techniques are critical to making Hybrid AI understand, interpret, generate, and manipulate human language. Hybrid AI uses two kinds of NLP techniques: NLU (Natural Language Understanding) and NLG (Natural Language Generation). NLU deals with the understanding and interpretation of human language inputs by machines, while NLG enables machines to create comprehensive and meaningful sentences.

5.2.5. Human Involvement and Integrative Processing

While we've touched on machine operations and algorithms, any understanding of Hybrid AI would be remiss without discussing the pivotal part of human involvement. Humans participate in system construction, algorithm optimization, decision-making, and even in real-time, extending the AI capabilities beyond its original programming boundaries. Typically overlooked is the process of integrative processing mechanisms, which combine machine-acquired knowledge with human inputs, leveraging the best of both to deliver enhanced performance.

5.3. Tools and Technologies

A variety of open-source and commercial tools are used in the making of Hybrid AI. These tools generally provide a conducive environment for developing, implementing, and maintaining ML models, and include software like TensorFlow, Caffe, Theano, Keras, PyTorch, and commercial software like Google Cloud ML Engine, Azure Machine Learning, and IBM Watson.

With the right mix of technically adroit human intellect, advanced ML algorithms, DL architectures, and NLP techniques, a Hybrid AI seamlessly couples the quantitative ability and speed of machines with the qualitative insights and experience of humans. Like a well-conducted orchestra, it integrates the strengths and mitigates the weaknesses of both.

As we peel back more layers of technological advances, understand that Hybrid AI isn't just an amalgamation of complex codes or sophisticated algorithms. Instead, it is a cohesive entity capable of learning, adapting, predicting, and innovating. Awareness of its technical facets not only demystifies the prevailing misconceptions surrounding AI but also lays a foundation for appreciating the potential of this transformative paradigm. Novel applications and innovations continue to surface as we cross new frontiers in this exciting journey of harmonizing machine and human intelligence.

Chapter 6. Building Bridges: Harmonizing Machine Logic and Human Reasoning

Achieving balance between machine logic and human reasoning is no small feat. Machine logic, marked by structured sequences of operations and data-driven decision-making, starkly contrasts with the fluid, intuitive, and context-driven nature of human reasoning. Bridging these two entities involves mapping the complex web of human cognition onto a mathematically coherent framework that machines can process. The harmonization process is as fascinating as it is challenging, involving research in artificial intelligence (AI), psychology, neuroscience, and computation theory.

6.1. The Theory of Cognition and Computation

Understanding the foundational concepts of cognition and computation is essential in marching towards the end goal of harmonizing machine logic and human reasoning. Cognition, in human terms, involves perception, learning, memory, and decision making. The human brain, a stew of billions of neurons and trillions of synapses, facilitates this complex dance, constantly perceiving, interpreting, and reacting to the environment.

Computation, on the other hand, involves executing a list of well-defined instructions to achieve a specific goal or solution. Each step is logical, structured, and devoid of intuition or emotion. The natural intelligence of humans and the artificial intelligence of machines function on fundamentally different principles, requiring a significant bridge to harmonize the two.

Machine learning algorithms tried to bridge this gap to some extent by allowing machines to 'learn' from data. Yet, their ability to reason and conceptualize like humans is still a far-cry from reality. The advent of Hybrid AI promises to lead us down this exciting and challenging pathway.

6.2. Decoding the Human Brain: Neuroscientific Insights into Cognition

Before transposing human cognition onto the computational matrix, we must first unravel the mysteries of the human brain. Fortunately, modern fields like computational neuroscience and cognitive science are making strides in this area. These disciplines break down cognitive processes into computationally tractable problems, enabling artificial neural networks to mimic aspects of human reasoning.

Functional magnetic resonance imaging (fMRI), for instance, helps in understanding how different parts of the brain interact when performing specific tasks, lending insight into the intricate workings of cognition. For example, the prefrontal cortex, the seat of higher-order cognitive functions, plays a crucial role in decision-making, planning, and social behavior.

6.3. The Arithmetic of Reasoning: Transposing Cognition onto Computation

Transposing human reasoning onto a computational framework, called cognitive computing, is the next pivotal step. This process necessitates the development of cognitive architectures that mimic the mind's various components and their interconnections. Such architectures ought to not only execute tasks efficiently, like machines, but also 'understand', reason, and learn like humans.

Cognitive architectures, like the Cognitive Architecture for Learning (CAL), are designed to simulate human cognition. CAL, for instance, learns from its environment, forms associations, makes predictions, and even exhibits creativity to some extent. By replicating the dynamism of human cognition, such architectures are critical in the pursuit of harmonizing machine logic and human reasoning.

Deep learning models like transformers and recurrent neural networks (RNNs) have emerged as powerful tools to mimic temporal dynamics of human cognition—an aspect notoriously difficult to capture in traditional models. These models have been instrumental in significant advancements in Natural Language Processing (NLP) and computer vision as they can comprehend nuances and subtleties akin to human intelligence.

6.4. Rationalizing the Machine: Imparting Human-Like Reasoning

As important as capturing human reasoning in machines is, it's equally essential that these machines exhibit 'rational' behavior. While machines can crunch numbers and sort data with breakneck speed and precision, they usually don't 'understand' the implications of their results. This limitation restricts machines to a predefined set of operations, causing them to stumble when faced with unforeseen inputs or circumstances.

To combat this, researchers are developing interpretive models and explainable AI (XAI) that can rationalize their results in ways humans can understand. Consequently, these developments will make AI more transparent, trustworthy, and transferable to real-world scenarios.

6.5. The Machine-Human Bridge: Hybrid AI

The fusion of machine logic and human reasoning in Hybrid AI must ensure smooth interaction between human intuition and machine precision. Apart from technologically advanced interfaces, a profound understanding of the ontological and epistemological differences between man and machine is of equal importance.

The construction of this 'bridge' involves creating machines capable of cognitive empathy—understanding, interpreting, and responding accurately to human emotions, intentions, and nuances, thus making machine-human interactions more natural, attentive, and adaptive. It further entails developing cognitive models that can be fine-tuned to an individual's learning pace, capacity, and style - a giant stride towards personalized AI.

When these elements gel perfectly, we'll witness AI not only mimicking human-like reasoning but also reflecting human-like emotions and empathic understanding—a significant leap towards true AI-human symbiosis. The harmonization of machine logic and human reasoning, thus, will spawn a new generation of AI, one that marries the best of both worlds: the analytical prowess of AI and the emotional intellect of humans.

In sum, Hybrid AI is more than a novel concept—it is a doorway to unprecedented possibilities, heralding an era where machine intelligence works proactively rather than reactively. This new breed of AI will partner with humans, augmenting our abilities, and fundamentally, unveiling unlimited potential for innovation, growth and wellbeing.

Chapter 7. Diverse Facets: Applications of Hybrid AI in Modern World

Hybrid AI systems, essentially, leverage the best of both artificial and human intelligence, offering wide-ranging applications that are being utilized in various sectors of our modern world. By combining the precision, speed, and unwavering focus of machine learning models with the human-like intuition, judgment, and creativity, Hybrid AI delivers solutions that are both efficient and effective, bearing a striking resemblance to human-like intelligence.

7.1. Commercial Applications of Hybrid AI

Businesses across the world are increasingly harnessing the proliferating power of Hybrid AI to drive business growth, optimize processes, and make prudent decisions. Financial sectors especially have recognized the value of such applications; using Hybrid AI for risk management and fraud detection. Instead of relying solely on rule-based systems which can overlook nuanced or complex fraud patterns, a hybrid approach can adapt, learn, and detect anomalous behavior with greater precision.

Retail businesses are also leveraging Hybrid AI for personalized customer experiences. Traditional recommendation systems solely dependent on machine learning algorithms can at times recommend irrelevant products, failing to understand the context. However, by incorporating human-like understanding into these algorithms, Hybrid AI enables a more contextual and personalized customer journey.

In marketing, Hybrid AI is used to analyze the effectiveness of campaigns, monitor customer sentiments across various platforms, and generate actionable insights. It's able to better understand human emotions, sarcasm, or cultural references, providing a closer-to-human understanding of market dynamics.

7.2. Health and Medical Fields

In the medical and healthcare sector, Hybrid AI has the potential to elevate the field to unprecedented scales. Patient care is one area where this becomes particularly valuable. Machine learning models can predict disease progression and suggest possible treatments. When integrated with doctors' experience and judgment, this can lead to more accurate diagnoses and personalized treatment plans.

Medical research is another area where the combination of human skills and artificial intelligence is generating incredible results. As the automated algorithms sift through multitudes of medical databases, research papers, and clinical reports, researchers can focus on interpreting these insights for practical applications, thereby accelerating the pace of medical discoveries.

7.3. Education and Learning

Education is another industry where the potential of Hybrid AI is being unleashed to great effect. In eLearning, Hybrid AI can monitor a student's progress, understand their learning patterns, pace, and proficiency levels. Subsequently, it can provide personalized content, instantly adapt to the individual's needs, and provide educators with real-time updates on a student's progress.

Language learning, in particular, benefits considerably from Hybrid AI. Learning a new language is a multidimensional task that needs the understanding of culture, context, and nuances. While traditional language learning applications can teach vocabulary or grammar,

Hybrid AI can understand and instruct linguistic nuances, context, and cultural understanding, making language learning more effective and engaging.

7.4. Defense and Cybersecurity

The defense sector is tapping into the power of Hybrid AI, using it for surveillance, anomaly detection, and predictive analysis to maintain security. It also plays a vast role in predictive maintenance of military equipment.

In cybersecurity, Hybrid AI offers to combat increasingly sophisticated cyber threats. Machine learning algorithms can scan and analyze vast amounts of data for potential threats, while human intellect discerns real threats from false positives and adapts the system for better future response.

7.5. Sustainability and Environmental Conservation

Hybrid AI is mobilizing change in sustainability and environmental conservation. AI systems can analyze vast amounts of data relating to climate change, biodiversity loss, pollution, and more. Experts, utilizing their understanding of environmental complexities, can interpret this data, design solutions and implement them more effectively.

These applications, while expansive, merely scratch the surface of Hybrid AI's potential role in our modern world. As technology continues to evolve and more industries recognize the achievable synergies of machine learning and human intellect, Hybrid AI's influence will only intensify. Documenting these developments, harnessing them and understanding their implications is vital for any enterprise seeking to gain a competitive edge in their respective market, ultimately shaping a future that speaks of commendable progress, fueled by a remarkable blend of human and artificial intelligence.

Chapter 8. Case Studies: Successful Implementations of Hybrid AI

As the technology leaps ahead at an unprecedented speed, hybrid artificial intelligence (AI) systems are increasingly being adopted in a variety of domains. Their ability to leverage the perfect blend of human intelligence and machine learning has led to several successful implementations. In this chapter, we will dive into some of these successful implementations, understand their workings, and draw valuable insights from their operations.

8.1. Google's AlphaGo: A Revolution in Strategy Gaming

One of the most celebrated applications of hybrid AI came in the domain of strategy gaming through Google's DeepMind creation, AlphaGo. The game of Go, an ancient East Asian strategic board game, is known for its complex gameplay which is said to have more possibilities than the total number of atoms in the universe.

In 2016, AlphaGo shocked the Go community worldwide when it defeated the world champion Go player, Lee Sedol, in a five-match tournament. Combining vast machine learning technologies, including neural networks and Monte Carlo tree searching methods, with human introspection in the form of training input from several skilled Go players, AlphaGo was a true manifestation of hybrid AI.

This event marked a monumental development for AI, proving that the combination of human strategic skills and machine's analytical capacity can tackle unprecedented challenges.

8.2. IBM's Watson: A Companion Physician

Another transformative case study that demonstrates the potential of hybrid AI is IBM's Watson Health. It is designed to offer comprehensive decision support for healthcare professionals, providing data-driven insights into diagnosis and treatment procedures.

Watson's knowledge base encompasses vast databases of medical literature, clinical guidelines, and research, which it periodically updates. It uses machine learning algorithms and natural language processing to uncover relevant information from diverse sources, several of which might be overlooked because of their vast number.

At the same time, Watson heavily depends on human expertise. Its training involves curating data by experienced medical practitioners and enhancing its insight-generating capacity through repeated exposure to real-world clinical scenarios. Watson melds machine learning capabilities with human-like comprehension of language and decision-making, resulting in an invaluable tool for healthcare.

8.3. Airbus's Skywise: Combining AI and Human Insights for Aviation Safety

Safety stands paramount in aviation. Airbus's Skywise is an example of how hybrid AI can drastically transform safety mechanisms in aviation. Skywise mines vast data from Airbus's various partners in the aviation industry, making cognitive use of AI for predictive maintenance to avoid potential malfunctions or even catastrophic failures.

The application of hybrid AI takes the process of data validation, aggregation, and interpretation to the next level, culminating in an intellectual system that can predict failure before it happens. Still, Skywise requires regular human intervention to analyze and assess the normative use of these predictions. Experts curate and train the AI to improve its predictions over time, making it a unique mix of AI and human insights.

8.4. Automated Trading Systems: Financial Market Predictions

Automated trading bots, which employ a hybrid mix of AI and human insights to predict financial market trends and automatically execute trade orders, are becoming increasingly popular. These systems use complex machine learning algorithms and statistical modeling to predict market trends and identify trading opportunities.

Traders and financial analysts offer their expert insights and investment strategies, train these bots with historical market trends, and fine-tune their predictive behavior. The personalized touch of human intelligence combined with machine's computational abilities and speed greatly enhance the accuracy and timeliness in trading, making these systems yet another promising implementation of hybrid AI.

8.5. Conclusion

Hybrid AI continues to redefine the boundaries of technological capabilities by aptly combining human intelligence and machine learning. Examples of successful implementations in various fields, from finance and healthcare to gaming and aviation, all resonate with the vast potential of hybrid AI.

As we move toward an increasingly digital future, the role of hybrid

AI technologies continues to expand, creating new realms of opportunity and application. While we have looked into a few case studies in this chapter, there is an abundance of successful implementations in the real world.

The saga of hybrid AI's evolution is far from over, and as it continues to develop and mature, one can expect the introduction of even more hybrid AI systems in our lives. Consequently, this will enrich the relationship between humans and machines while opening up new paths for innovation, creativity, and productivity.

Chapter 9. Cyber Ethics: Contemplating the Moral Landscape of Hybrid AI

The intertwining of advanced machines and human intelligence promised by Hybrid AI raises numerous ethical dilemmas that need to be thoroughly examined, ensuring safe, sustainable, and beneficial evolution of this exciting technology.

9.1. Exploring the Ethical Concerns

Firstly, we must address the key ethical questions evoked by Hybrid AI. Whose morals should these advanced systems adhere to? How can we ensure that the AI knows when to defer to human judgement in decision-making processes?

Let's consider a hypothetical scenario: a Hybrid AI system functioning as an autonomous vehicle. This vehicle finds itself in a predicament where an accident is inevitable. Now the question arises: should the vehicle's AI prioritize the safety of its passengers or the pedestrians? There are no right or wrong answers to this conundrum. The ethical decisions we program into these machines will reflect the moral compass of their human architects.

Another concern is the potential for misuse or exploitation. Given the comprehensive abilities of Hybrid AI, the risk of these systems being used for ill-intentioned purposes cannot be disregarded. Clear directives regarding ethical use and stringent restrictions must be established to prevent potential exploitation and ensure the technology serves the greater good.

9.2. Navigating in the Ocean of Data Privacy

The development of Hybrid AI inherently demands extensive data as nourishment to grow, evolve, and function optimally. Personal data, such as behaviour, preferences, and even biometric information, might be an invaluable resource for these systems to learn and improve. However, who owns this data, and who determines how it's used or shared are complicated issues to resolve.

Data encapsulates more than just informational entities; It represents individual identity, autonomy, and potentially, privacy. Therefore, strict guidelines for data collection, storage, and usage must be implemented, ensuring the user's privacy is not compromised. Furthermore, informed consent and transparency must be the foundational stones in building a healthy relationship of trust between the user and the technology.

9.3. The Balance: Autonomy and Dependancy

As Hybrid AI evolves, it naturally assumes an increasingly dominant role in the decision-making process, and we risk becoming dependent on these AI systems. Would such dependency counterproductively lead to a decrease in our decision-making capacities? This dependence potentially threatens our autonomy and free will from being usurped by machine intelligence. Striking the right balance between utilizing the capabilities of Hybrid AI and maintaining our autonomy is a daunting, yet crucial task.

9.4. Inclusion and Accessibility

Technology should be a democratizing tool, leading to an inclusive and equitable society. However, in reality, often advanced technologies like Hybrid AI can accentuate social inequities if not designed and distributed thoughtfully. Everyone should have access to, and benefit from, Hybrid AI irrespective of their gender, socioeconomic status, race, or place of origin.

Aspectually, individuals with varying levels of tech-savviness should all be able to interact with and benefit from this technology. Essentially, Hybrid AI should be a tool that empowers all humankind, not just a select privileged few.

9.5. The Ownership Dilemma

Finally, who owns and controls these hyperintelligent systems remains unresolved. Essentially, should corporations, governments, or individual creators hold ownership rights over these creations? The prospect of monopolized control over such powerful technology can stir unease and fear, possibly leading to significant social disparity and power imbalances. Collective ownership or some form of equitable distribution could mitigate such risks.

Hybrid AI deeply entwines with our human experience, making it imperative to contemplate and address these ethical issues methodically and carefully. Respect for human rights, strict data protection laws, transparency, and informed consent should underpin this technology's evolution. Global cooperation ensuring the widespread education on the ethical use of AI, stringent legislation, and technical safeguards will fortify humanity's journey into this fascinating new era of Hybrid AI.

In conclusion, the moral landscape of Hybrid AI is complex and vast, yet traversing it is crucial to responsibly benefit from the limitless potential of what may be humanity's most significant technological achievement.

Chapter 10. Future Potential: Exploring the Uncharted Terrains of Hybrid AI

The continuous cycle of technological advancement and innovation has set us off towards a path in the Artificial Intelligence (AI) landscape where machines no longer operate as solitary entities. This evolution, embodying the best of human-like cognition with machine capabilities, is what we call Hybrid AI. The future is rich with potential and the scope for further development seems boundless.

10.1. Evolution of AI: From Traditional to Hybrid

AI began with rule-based systems that could perform simple tasks. As time passed, machine learning models were introduced, with computers taking in data, learning from it, and predicting outcomes. However, these systems were purely computational and had no 'human touch'. This is where Hybrid AI steps in, integrating human-like cognition into machine intelligence. Understanding this evolutionary journey helps us anticipate what might lie ahead, as history often serves as a template for the future.

Machine learning and reasoning, human-AI collaboration, and multidimensional AI scaling are the three pillars of Hybrid AI. Each of these pillars holds a significant future, reflective of formidable potential for growth, improvements, and innovations. Discussions in the following sections will delve into these.

10.2. Machine Learning and Reasoning: The Dynamic Duo

At the core of Hybrid AI lies machine learning and machine reasoning. Machine learning relies on analytics, pattern identification and statistical modeling to predict outcomes. Machine reasoning, however, uses logical reasoning to infer, plan and make decisions. This duo, when adeptly combined within Hybrid AI, expands the technology's potential.

In the future, the integration may well develop to a point where machines are capable of not just learning and reasoning from data, but also extrapolating from it using semantic cognition, much the same way as humans do. Sophisticated algorithms are in the works, destined to spur machine abilities to comprehend, analyze, and synthesize novel situations. This promises an unprecedented level of automation across diverse industries, presenting tangible and far-reaching impacts.

10.3. Human-AI Collaboration: Co-Existence and Co-Evolution

AI systems have often been seen in a competitive lens with respect to human intellect. However, Hybrid AI drives a different narrative, offering a symbiotic relationship between human intelligence and artificial intellect.

This core tenet of Hybrid AI proposes an interesting future where machines could potentially serve as intellectual partners to humans. They could help in overcoming cognitive biases, enhance decision-making skills, even inspire creativity and innovation. This partnership's future is tantalizing, heralding an era where our machines may become intellectual counterparts rather than just tools for simplification.

Moreover, it is also worth noting how Hybrid AI could lead to the democratization of AI technology, empowering individuals and organizations to leverage it without requiring extensive expertise in data science, consequently bridging social and economic gaps.

10.4. Multidimensional AI Scaling: Addressing the Complexity of Reality

Traditional AI has often been found wanting in understanding the complex nuances of real-world data. That's because reality is multi-dimensional and massively scattered, something AI systems are generally not programmed to understand. This is where Hybrid AI can apply multidimensional scaling to create more robust AI systems.

This new approach could lead to AI scaling in multiple dimensions, handling complex, real-time scenarios effortlessly. High-dimensional states encompassing economic, political, societal, cultural, and personal aspects could be leveraged more effectively, benighting to groundbreaking applications affecting numerous sectors and lives.

10.5. Imagining Scenario-Specific Explorations

Let's reflect upon specific areas where Hybrid AI's future potential can be explored.

10.5.1. Healthcare: Crafting Healthier Tomorrows

AI has already made substantial inroads in healthcare, from diagnosing diseases to developing new drugs. With Hybrid AI, these applications could be further advanced. Hybrid AI-based systems could learn and reason from pre-existing health data and make nuanced decisions. They could also actively collaborate with doctors and researchers, leading to personalized healthcare plans resulting in better wellbeing for many.

10.5.2. Education: Personalizing Wisdom

Education stands to benefit notably from Hybrid AI. Future systems could adapt to individual learning habitats and styles, providing personalized education for all, regardless of background or abilities. Education could transform from a one-size-fits-all model to one that is as unique as every learner.

10.5.3. Business: Reinventing Industries

Hybrid AI can overhaul current business paradigms, offering businesses intelligent support in decision-making, forecasting, and analytics. Businesses could harvest the power of Hybrid AI to customize customer experiences and drive growth. The implications could revolutionize industries, opening novel markets, and creating fresh opportunities.

10.6. Embracing Challenges: Understanding Limitations

While the future potential appears immensely promising, understanding Hybrid AI's limitations is equally crucial. Maintaining the balance between human intelligence and machine learning requires careful calibration. Concerns regarding ethical implications, data privacy, and job loss call for robust regulatory frameworks. Innovative solutions to these challenges will ignite remarkable future pathways for Hybrid AI's evolution.

In conclusion, the advancement toward Hybrid AI's future potentials carries monumental significance, wielding the power to shape our interactions with technology and even alter the ideological fabric of our society. As we anticipate this transformative future, it is not just the discovery of uncharted terrains but also the learning and the journey itself that will indelibly inform and shape our world. What we need to remember as we undertake this exploration is that Hybrid AI is not about human versus machine, but rather a harmonious convergence of the two.

Chapter 11. Conclusion: The Journey Ahead in the Hybridized AI Landscape

Architecting the future with Hybrid AI offers an unprecedented opportunity to shape our societies and economies in empowering ways. We're now the travelers and explorers of a digital frontier richly inhabited by algorithms, machine intelligence, and the expertise of human cognition in a partnership that is still in its infancy.

11.1. Synergizing Human and Machine Intelligence

While traditional AI models rely solely on vast amounts of data to make decisions, Hybrid AI leverages human intervention when necessary, making the underlying decision-making process more explainable and transparent. This blend of human cognizance and machine efficiency introduces a profound shift in our understanding of AI, embodying the ideology of 'intelligence augmentation' wherein machines complement human intelligence rather than replace it.

This augury calls for the embracement of the paradoxical: the union of the organic and the algorithmic, the instinctive and the calculated. This hybridization produces an intelligence that is fundamentally different from its constituents, taking the best from both the human and the AI territory.

11.2. Unleashing the Potential of Hybrid AI

Hybrid AI presents itself as a solution to the limitations inherent in pure forms of AI. By introducing an element of human judgment into the traditionally purely algorithm-driven AI process, it brings unprecedented granularity and flexibility into the machine learning process.

With the maturity of Hybrid AI, industries will be able to enjoy the best of both worlds, which was previously unachievable with either purely human or artificial decision making systems. It has the potential to bring agility in decision-making, continuous learning from feedback, and the aptitude to adapt in variable environments.

As we unlock more potential from this synergy, more businesses and organizations may be in a better position to navigate uncertainty, manage risks, and drive consistent growth.

11.3. Uncharted Horizons and Unforeseen Challenges

There are, however, a host of challenges that yet await us in the Hybrid AI landscape. Important issues need to be addressed, such as the definition of appropriate boundaries for machine autonomy in making decisions, possible disalignment of goals between incentives for machine learning and human interests, and data privacy concerns. It is crucial to be cognizant of these challenges as we initiate our journey in this new AI era.

Moreover, policies and guidelines to regulate hybrid AI systems will need to be developed to prevent potential misuse. These guidelines will ensure the ethical use of AI and protect fundamental human rights. Since these AI technologies continuously evolve, adaptive regulation will be needed.

11.4. Embracing Hybrid AI as an Imperative for Future Innovation

Today, the integration of human and machine intelligence is more than just a next step in AI; it's a watershed moment in the march towards harnessing the combined power of humans and machines to innovate and solve complex problems.

As more and more organizations embark on their Hybrid AI journey, they will need to ensure that they're not merely adopting a sound technical approach to integrate AI, but also a cultural willingness to embrace AI.

With Hybrid AI, we no longer have to yearn for a distant future where AI can perfectly emulate human cognitive faculties. Instead, we can focus on creating better techniques for humans and AI to collaborate, improving the performance of both, and thereby elevating the potential for innovation.

In conclusion, the journey toward Hybrid AI has just started and is positively brimming with possibility. One can think of it as the dawn of a new age — a liminal zone where the frontier between human and machine blurs. Hybrid AI signifies stepping into uncharted territories of cognitive collaboration that offer the thrilling prospect of expanding our collective problem-solving capacities, constantly reminding us the strength in our diversity.

The journey ahead is undeniably fraught with challenges, but beyond them lie the data-rich plains of opportunity. As pioneers on this journey, it is our responsibility to steer Hybrid AI with thoughtful intent, nudging it to empower all stakeholders in a sustainable, ethical, and equitable manner.

www.ingramcontent.com/pod-product-compliance
Lightning Source LLC
LaVergne TN
LVHW051626050326
832903LV00033B/4689